4/10

Ships

Emily Bone
Designed by Jessica Johnson

Illustrated by Colin King

Additional design by Helen Edmonds, Nick Wakeford and John Russell
Reading consultant: Alison Kelly, Roehampton University
Ship consultant: Denis Stonham

Contents

Little and large

Ships are all shapes and sizes, and are used to carry lots of different things.

This is an oil tanker. It carries oil to countries around the world.

Some oil tankers are so big that people use bicycles to move around on them.

Ship power

Ships have been used for a very long time.

Thousands of years ago, people paddled along rivers in hollowed-out logs.

The Ancient Egyptians built ships from reeds to carry gold, food and spices.

The Vikings sailed over rough seas in tough wooden ships called longships.

In Ancient China, ships called junks, like this one, carried hundreds of passengers.

Vikings carved fierce wooden beasts onto the front of their ships to scare their enemies.

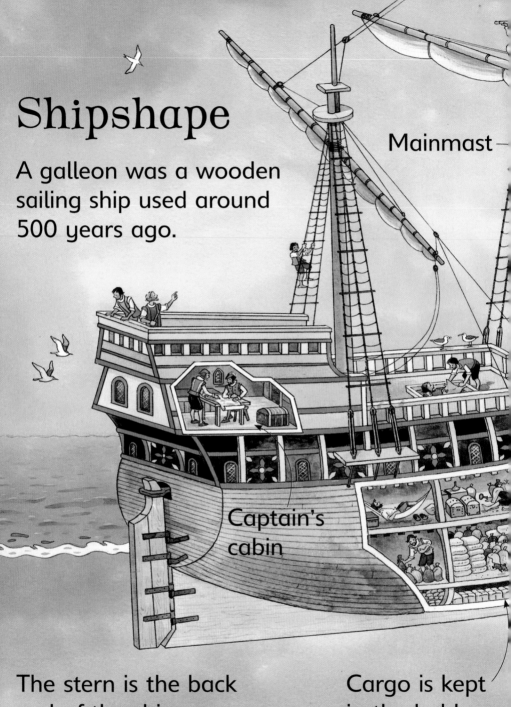

Shipshape

A galleon was a wooden sailing ship used around 500 years ago.

Mainmast

Captain's cabin

The stern is the back end of the ship.

Cargo is kept in the hold.

6

Upper deck

Hull

The front of the hull is called the bow.

The galley is the ship's kitchen.

Anchor

The side of this galleon has been cut away so that you can see below the deck.

7

A sailor's life

Over a hundred sailors worked on ships such as galleons. There were lots of jobs to do.

A navigator mapped out the ship's route across the sea.

A lookout stood on a high platform and watched for danger.

A team of sailors repaired the sails and ropes.

The cook was often a sailor who had been injured.

The captain was in charge of a ship. This is Ferdinand Magellan, a famous captain and explorer who sailed in the 1500s.

Fighting ships

Warships fought battles at sea. Ship captains had clever ways of sinking enemy ships.

A trireme was an ancient Greek warship with a spike on the front.

The spike was used to punch a big hole in the side of the enemy's ship.

In this painting of a battle in 1745, the ships are firing cannons at each other.

The cannons on galleons fired heavy metal balls that could wreck another ship.

Fireships were old galleons that were set on fire and sailed into enemy ships.

Pirate attack

Pirates were robbers who captured ships and stole their cargo.

This painting shows a pirate with lots of weapons and treasure.

Pirates lived on small, fast ships called sloops.

1. If pirates spotted a ship they chased it, until they caught up with it.

2. They fired their cannons to try and make the ship's crew surrender.

3. The pirates boarded the ship and took things such as gold and jewels.

4. They sometimes kept the ship and set the crew adrift in a small boat.

There were a few women pirates who disguised themselves as men to be allowed on board.

Sails for speed

Clippers were sailing ships that carried tea and other cargo quickly over long distances.

A clipper's narrow hull cut through the waves much quicker than wider ships.

Some clippers raced each other. The captain of the fastest ship won a prize.

This is the Cutty Sark, a clipper that carried tea from China to England in the 1800s.

More than 30 huge sails caught the wind and pushed the clipper along.

Full steam ahead

Steamships were even faster than clippers. They had sails and engines that gave the ship extra power.

This is the Great Eastern, a paddlesteamer built in 1858.

Coal was burned to boil water and make steam. The steam powered the engines.

The engines turned giant paddlewheels that pushed the ship through the water.

The Great Eastern had a propeller, too. This helped to push the ship along.

Later, engines became more powerful, so sails were only used in emergencies.

Titanic disaster

When the Titanic set sail on April 10th 1912, it was the biggest steamship ever built. Over 2,000 people were on board.

1. A crowd gathered to watch the Titanic leave the port at Southampton, UK.

2. Inside the ship, the passengers relaxed, slept and ate in luxury.

3. One night, a lookout spotted an iceberg, but it was too late to avoid it.

4. The Titanic hit the iceberg, ripping huge holes along the hull.

Water rushed into the ship and dragged it under the sea.

The Titanic sank and broke in two. Only 700 people were rescued.

Building and repairs

When ships need to be cleaned or repaired they go into a huge drained area next to the sea, called a drydock.

1. A dirty ship sails into the drydock for essential cleaning and repairs.

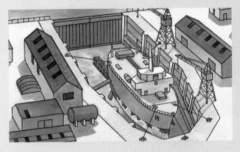

2. The drydock's big gates are shut and fastened, and the water is pumped out.

3. Seaweed and dirt are scraped off the ship and the hull is repainted.

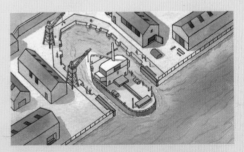

4. Water is pumped into the dock, the gates are opened and the ship floats out.

Ships are always built near the sea. This is a ship being built in 1941.

At the port

When ships reach land, they load and unload cargo at a port.

Container ships carry cargo in truck-sized boxes all over the world. Huge cranes lift the heavy containers on and off the ship.

Tugs are small boats that help guide the ship into port.

Roll-on, roll-off ferries carry people, cars and trucks from one place to another.

Vehicles arrive at a port. They drive up a large ramp, into the ferry.

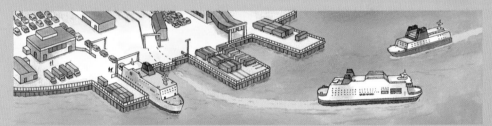

They drive to a parking space inside. The door is closed and the ferry sets sail.

When the ferry reaches land, a door opens and the vehicles drive off.

Studying the sea

Scientists study the sea and the things living in it from ships.

This is a Deep Rover. Scientists can lower it from a ship and travel underwater in it.

Some ships have underwater robots that scientists use to explore deep under the sea.

The robot is lowered into the water from the ship.

A camera on the robot sends pictures to scientists on board the ship.

The scientists send signals to the robot to move its arms and collect samples.

Icy waters

In very cold places, such as Antarctica, the sea freezes into ice. This makes it difficult for ships to sail there.

A ship called an icebreaker clears a path for other ships to sail through the ice.

The icebreaker's strong metal bow rises up over the ice.

The front of the ship presses down onto the ice and breaks it.

The ship behind can sail safely through the clear water.

To keep wildlife safe, only a hundred visitors are allowed to land on Antarctica at one time.

Working on the waves

Some ships are built to do special jobs.

This is an aircraft carrier. It is a huge ship with a runway for planes to take off and land.

Some ships carry very large objects. This is a wrecked ship being taken to be repaired.

Liners are floating hotels with pools and shops on board.

On a factory ship, fish are caught, prepared and frozen.

Some aircraft carriers can carry up to 90 planes and a crew of over 3,000 people.

Glossary of ship words

Here are some of the words in this book you might not know. This page tells you what they mean.

 mast - a long pole on a ship that holds up the sails.

 cargo - the things that a ship carries from place to place.

 hold - an area of a ship where cargo is kept.

 deck - a floor on a ship. Some ships have lots of decks.

 hull - the main body of a ship, usually made from wood or metal.

 crew - the people who work on a ship, led by the captain.

 dock - ships load and unload cargo and are built and repaired here.

Websites to visit

You can visit exciting websites to find out more about ships.

To visit these websites, go to the Usborne Quicklinks Website at **www.usborne-quicklinks.com** Read the internet safety guidelines, and then type the keywords "**beginners ships**".

The websites are regularly reviewed and the links in Usborne Quicklinks are updated. However, Usborne Publishing is not responsible, and does not accept liability, for the content or availability of any website other than its own. We recommend that children are supervised while on the internet.

There is a place on this ship for a helicopter to take off and land.

Index

Acknowledgements

Photo credits
The publishers are grateful to the following for permission to reproduce material:
© Arco Images GmbH/Alamy 26; © Bettmann/CORBIS 21; © Bill Brooks/Alamy cover background;
© Delaware Art Museum, Wilmington, USA/The Bridgeman Art Library 12;
© Getty Images 5, 14-15; © Joel W. Rogers/CORBIS cover; © Jon Mitchell/Topfoto 28;
© Mark Deeble & Victoria Stone/OSF/Photolibrary 24;
© National Maritime Museum, Greenwich, London 10-11;
© Patrick Bennett/Age Fotostock/Photolibrary 2-3; © Portuguese Maritime Museum 9;
© Science Museum Library 16-17;
© Steve Bloom Images/Alamy 31; © Steve Mason/Photodisc/Photolibrary 1;
© www.containershipping.nl 22 (Michael van der Meer).

Every effort has been made to trace and acknowledge ownership of copyright. If any rights have
been omitted, the publishers offer to rectify this in any subsequent editions following notification.